super spiralized

fresh & delicious ways to use your spiralizer

Orathay Souksisavanh & Vania Nikolcic

Photography by Charlotte Lascève

hardie grant books

contents

cutting implements

Here are a few very useful pieces of equipment for shaping your favourite raw vegetables.
These easy-to-use implements will enable you to quickly turn all sorts of vegetables into juliennes, spaghetti, tagliatelle and thin strips. Create spectacular dishes and culinary displays worthy of a chef!

1 — MANDOLINE
Perfect for cutting raw or cooked vegetables into slices or strips.

2 — MULTIFUNCTIONAL JULIENNE PEELER
A multifunctional peeler with three interchangeable blades that will enable you to create vegetable strips, juliennes, spaghetti or tagliatelle.

3 — VEGETABLE PEELER
Very easy to use, small and handy, it serves not only for peeling vegetables but also for cutting them into strips or even slices. Perfect for slicing courgettes (zucchini), carrots, cucumbers and daikon.

4 — SPIRALIZER
This little pencil-sharpener-like implement can turn vegetables into long pieces of spaghetti — a revolutionary utensil!

multifunctional julienne peeler

With its three blades, this peeler is very easy to use and versatile.

THE STRAIGHT BLADE (1)
For creating strips and slices. In a few minutes, courgette (zucchini) ribbons can be ready to grill (broil) in the oven!

FINE JULIENNE BLADE (2)
For creating fine juliennes and vegetable spaghetti. Ideal for recipes that require thin strands of vegetables to use in parcels or salads, for example.

WIDE JULIENNE BLADE (3)
For making vegetable tagliatelle or thicker juliennes. Use this blade for fragile fruit or vegetables, such as avocado or mango.

A julienne peeler is perfect for courgettes, carrots and large radishes, such as daikon, but also for beetroot (beets) (choose long ones for a more spectacular result), squash, avocados and mangoes.

If the vegetable is very long, use the peeler lengthways to obtain good long ribbons or juliennes. If the vegetable is rounder in shape (e.g. potato, beetroot/beet, mango), work around it with the peeler in one steady movement to get the strips as long as possible.

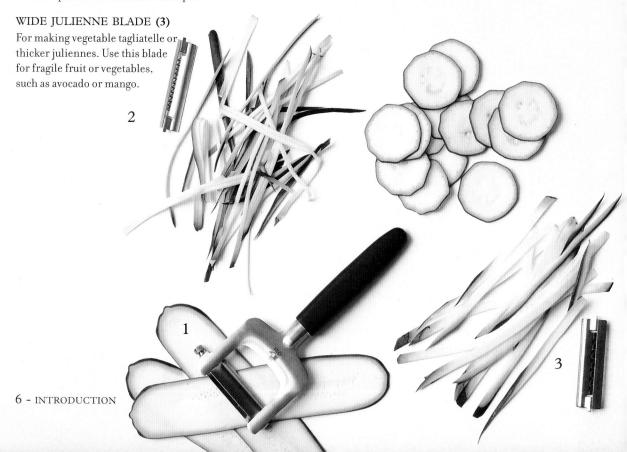

2

1

3

mandoline

The mandoline is used to cut raw vegetables into thin slices and works best when the vegetables are very firm. The forms you obtain will vary depending on the type of vegetable and the direction in which you slice it: long, rounded vegetables will yield strips or round slices; those comprising layers of leaves, such as leeks, cabbages and endives, will fall into thin strips.

Although the mandoline is easy to use, it's a good idea to hold the vegetables with the palm of your hand flat to avoid cutting yourself.

DIFFERENT TYPES OF MANDOLINE

The simplest version has a single blade. Very easy to handle, it is perfect for occasional use.

There are also more sophisticated mandolines – generally larger and a bit more expensive – that enable you to cut very fine slices and to precisely adjust the thickness of the slices.

spiralizer

This is the utensil that is revolutionalising vegetable cutting. Really simple and very original, it's used like a pencil sharpener. The simple handheld one shown below has a fine julienne fitting at one end to create spaghetti and a wider julienne fitting for creating ribbons at the other.

There are also more heavy-duty stand versions available. While they take up more space and cost more, this sort of spiralizer is worth the investment if you plan to use it on a regular basis as it's quick and easy to use and likely to have several different attachments.

For optimum results, it's best to use vegetables that are not too thick and above all that are relatively long. If they are too fat, they won't fit in the spiralizer; too short and they won't give you enough grip to turn them and they will yield only very short lengths of spaghetti. Courgettes (zucchini), carrots and sweet potatoes work perfectly.

To obtain long lengths of spaghetti, turn the vegetable (or the handle of the spiralizer on a stand model) smoothly, without jolting. The spaghetti will be endless! Perfect for creating all sorts of nests, impressive salads and alternative chips.

quick and easy ideas

SPIRALIZED VEGETABLE SOUP

SERVES 4
PREPARATION: 10 MINUTES
COOKING TIME: 20 MINUTES

1 chicken stock (broth) cube, 1 parsnip, 1 fat carrot, 1 fairly long potato, 1 leek (white part only), 3 celery sticks, 2 tablespoons olive oil, pepper, chopped chervil

1. Dissolve the stock cube in 1 litre (34 fl oz) boiling water.

2. Peel the parsnip, carrot and potato. Cut the leek in half, then use the mandoline to cut it into juliennes. Slice all the other vegetables using a julienne peeler.

3. Sweat all the vegetables in the oil over a low heat for 5 minutes. Add the hot stock and cook for a further 10–15 minutes.

4. Season with pepper and adjust the seasoning to taste. Serve hot, sprinkled with some chopped chervil.

TZATZIKI-STYLE CUCUMBER SPAGHETTI

SERVES 2 OR 3
PREPARATION: 5 MINUTES

1 cucumber, ½ bunch of mint, 1 small garlic clove, 250 g (9 oz) Greek-style yoghurt, 1 tablespoon white wine vinegar, 2 tablespoons olive oil, salt and pepper

1. Slice the cucumber using a julienne peeler.

2. Finely chop the mint and garlic and stir into the yoghurt. Season with the vinegar, oil, salt and pepper.

3. Place the cucumber spaghetti on the plates and pour over the minty yoghurt dressing.

COURGETTE TAGLIATELLE WITH PESTO

SERVES 4
PREPARATION: 10 MINUTES
COOKING TIME: 30 MINUTES

30 g (1 oz) pine nuts, 3 courgettes (zucchini), 1 small bunch basil, 2 garlic cloves, 1 tablespoon white wine vinegar, 100 ml (3½ fl oz) olive oil, 30 g (1 oz) grated Parmesan, salt and pepper

1. Toast the pine nuts in a dry frying pan (skillet). Wash the courgettes and basil.

2. Blend the garlic, basil, half the pine nuts, the vinegar, oil and Parmesan. Season with salt and pepper.

3. Cut the courgette into ribbons using a mandoline. Put them into a colander or sieve and plunge them into boiling water for 30 seconds. They should be al dente.

4. Drain the courgettes, lay them on a plate, pour over the pesto and serve sprinkled with the remaining pine nuts.

COURGETTE, FETA AND MINT FRITTATA

SERVES 2
PREPARATION: 5 MINUTES
COOKING TIME: 5 MINUTES

2 sprigs of mint, 1 courgette (zucchini), 2 tablespoons olive oil, 5 eggs, salt and pepper, 100 g (3½ oz) feta

1. Finely chop the mint and slice the courgette using a julienne peeler fitted with a fine julienne blade to create long spaghetti.

2. Heat the oil in a large frying pan (skillet), beat the eggs and pour them into the pan. Reduce the heat to minimum.

3. Add the courgette, season, then crumble in the feta. Cook over a low heat until the omelette begins to set. Add the mint. The frittata should remain slightly runny.

mango and smoked duck breast canapés

1 firm mango
60 g (2 oz) thinly sliced smoked
duck breast

sauce
2 tablespoons cider vinegar
1 tablespoon walnut oil
1 teaspoon honey
salt and pepper

1. Peel the mango. Peel the flesh using a julienne peeler fitted with a wide julienne blade, making the strips as long as you can.

2. Make a nest of mango on each skewer: push the skewer into one end of a mango strip and twist to wind it around the skewer. Twist and secure a slice of duck breast at the base of each mango nest. Repeat to make more skewers until you have used up all the mango and duck breast. Set aside in the fridge.

3. Prepare the sauce by mixing together the vinegar, oil and honey. Season to taste. Spoon a little sauce over each appetizer, or serve it separately as a dip.

avocado bruschetta

1 firm avocado
juice of ½ lemon
½ bunch of coriander (cilantro),
leaves picked
6 slices of rustic crusty bread
2 tomatoes, sliced
salt
1 small red onion, finely chopped
1 red chilli, thinly sliced and deseeded
fleur de sel
1 lime, quartered

1. Peel the avocado, remove the stone and slice the flesh into ribbons using a julienne peeler. Put the avocado in a bowl and sprinkle with lemon juice to prevent it turning brown. Gently stir in the chopped coriander.

2. Assemble the bruschetta, starting with the tomato slices. Sprinkle with salt, then add some onion and avocado. To finish, garnish with chilli slices and fleur de sel. Serve with the lime wedges.

vietnamese sandwiches

2 large chicken legs (thighs and
drumsticks), boneless if possible
200 g (7 oz) daikon (10 cm/4 in in length)
200 g (7 oz) carrots
½ cucumber
1 baguette
a few sprigs of coriander (cilantro)
3 tablespoons mayonnaise
strong liquid seasoning
pinch of chopped chilli, to taste
pepper

chicken marinade

20 g (¾ oz) lemongrass, finely chopped
thumb-sized piece fresh ginger,
finely chopped
3 garlic cloves, finely chopped
1 tablespoon fish sauce
1 teaspoon caster (superfine) sugar
½ teaspoon salt
½ teaspoon pepper

vegetable marinade

50 g (2 oz) caster (superfine) sugar
3 tablespoons rice wine vinegar
1 teaspoon salt
1 small chilli, finely chopped

1. Prepare the chicken by boning it if necessary.

2. Mix all the chicken marinade ingredients together. Put the chicken in a dish, pour over the marinade and turn to coat well. Leave to marinate overnight if possible.

3. The next day, preheat the grill (broiler). Peel the daikon and carrots, then shred using a julienne peeler fitted with a fine julienne blade.

4. Mix together the vegetable marinade ingredients, pour over the shredded daikon and carrot and leave to marinate for 15 minutes.

5. Meanwhile, grill (broil) the chicken until golden. Leave to cool, then cut into pieces.

6. Shred the cucumber using a julienne peeler.

7. Cut the baguette into three equal lengths, then cut lengthways into halves. Spread the mayonnaise over one half of each sandwich, arrange some pieces of chicken on top, then add a generous helping of marinated vegetables and some strips of cucumber. Add some coriander leaves, a little liquid seasoning, some pepper and a pinch of chopped chilli to taste. Serve immediately.

Chef's tips

It's handy to ask your butcher to bone the chicken legs for you.

Prepare the chicken in large quantities. Marinate, then freeze it for next time.

julienned vegetable tempura

½ celeriac
1 small head of celery
1 tablespoon plain (all-purpose) flour
½ packet of tempura mix (Asian grocery)
vegetable oil, for frying
sweet chilli sauce, to serve

1. Preheat a deep-fat fryer to 170°C (335°F).

2. Peel the celeriac and cut the celery sticks in half. Roughly chop the celery leaves and set aside.

3. Shred the celeriac and celery using a julienne peeler fitted with a fine julienne blade. Mix together in a large bowl. Add the flour and toss to coat the vegetables.

4. Prepare the tempura batter according to the packet instructions.

5. Put a small pile of shredded vegetables on a plate and lightly drizzle with tempura batter. Repeat until you have used up all the shredded vegetables and batter, then plunge the small piles into the hot oil, a few at a time. Remove the tempura from the oil when they begin to turn golden and drain on kitchen paper. Serve hot with some sweet chilli sauce.

Chef's tips

Drizzling only a little batter on the vegetables yields a light tempura with two different textures.

You can use all sorts of vegetables (carrots, sweet potatoes, turnips, asparagus, etc.) for this tempura.

vegetable spring rolls

1 large chicken breast
salt and pepper
2 tablespoons vegetable oil
1 cucumber
1 raw Chioggia beetroot (beet)
or red beetroot
10 small round rice paper sheets
1 lettuce heart, leaves separated
1 bunch of mint, leaves picked
hoisin sauce
1 bird's eye chilli (optional), deseeded
and finely chopped
1 tablespoon chopped peanuts (optional)

1. Season the chicken breast with salt and pepper and fry in the oil until golden.

2. Leave to cool, then cut into 5 mm- (¼ in-) thick slices.

3. Shred the cucumber and beetroot using a julienne peeler fitted with a fine julienne blade. Alternatively, you can use a spiralizer for the cucumber. Set aside.

4. Soak the rice paper sheets in cold water, then lay them on a board and fill them. With each sheet, start with a lettuce leaf, then add two or three mint leaves, some cucumber, some beetroot and two slices of chicken. Allow the filling to poke out of one side of the sheet. Roll up the sheets tightly, cutting off any excess rice paper at the bottom of the roll.

5. Pour some hoisin sauce into a small bowl and stir in the chilli and peanuts. Serve the spring rolls with the hoisin sauce.

Chef's tips

If you are not serving the rolls straight away, place them on a plate, cover them with a clean, damp cloth and store them in the fridge. This will prevent them from drying out.

Vary the vegetables you use to fill the rolls (shredded daikon, carrot, celery etc.). You could even include fruit (mango, green apple, avocado etc.) and prawns (shrimp), duck breast or smoked salmon. The choice is yours!

For an alternative dipping sauce, try the dressing on page 36.

potato balls

6 long potatoes
3 garlic cloves
1 sprig of thyme
salt and pepper
vegetable oil, for frying
a few sprigs of flat-leaf parsley, leaves
finely chopped
150 g (5 oz) fromage frais

1. Peel the largest potato and cook it in boiling water with the garlic and thyme. Drain, peel the garlic and discard the thyme. Mash the potato and garlic together and season generously with salt and pepper. Leave to cool.

2. Preheat a deep-fat fryer to 170°C (335°F). Peel the remaining potatoes, then rinse and dry them. Shred them using a spiralizer. To keep the pieces as long as possible, turn the potatoes slowly and steadily.

3. Form the garlic mash into small balls. Wind the potato spaghetti around each ball.

4. Carefully plunge the balls, a few at a time, into the hot oil and cook until golden. Drain on kitchen paper.

5. In a bowl, stir the chopped parsley into the fromage frais. Season generously and serve this sauce with the potato balls.

matchstick chips with rosemary

3 large potatoes
vegetable oil, for frying
2 sprigs of rosemary, leaves picked
coarse salt

1. Preheat a deep-fat fryer to 180°C (350°F). Peel the potatoes, then rinse and dry. Shred them lengthways using a julienne peeler.

2. Carefully plunge the julienned potatoes into the hot oil. When the potato starts to turn golden, add the rosemary leaves to the oil.

3. When the matchstick chips are golden, drain them and serve with some coarse salt.

Chef's tip
These matchstick chips are great served with roast chicken or meat but are also good on their own with apéritifs.

vegetable röstis

600 g (1 lb 3 oz) potatoes, peeled
250 g (9 oz) butternut squash (pumpkin),
peeled and deseeded
2 onions, finely chopped
½ bunch of flat-leaf parsley, roughly
chopped
salt and pepper
vegetable oil

1. Shred the potatoes and butternut squash using a julienne peeler. Put in a bowl and add the chopped onion and half the chopped parsley. Season with salt and pepper and mix to combine.

2. Heat some oil in a frying pan (skillet). Take a handful of the julienne mixture and press it together in your hands to form a fairly thick patty. Repeat until you have used up all the mixture.

3. Gently lower the patties, a few at a time, into the hot oil. Carefully turn them over when the edges begin to turn golden. Add more oil to the pan for subsequent batches if necessary.

4. Drain the röstis on kitchen paper, then serve hot, sprinkled with the remaining chopped parsley.

Chef's tip

You can replace the butternut squash with sweet potato or parsnip if you wish, but you will need to keep the potato as the starch it contains serves to bind the ingredients together.

grilled vegetable salad

2 red (bell) peppers (or 1 packet of frozen grilled/broiled peppers)
2 very firm aubergines (eggplants)
3 courgettes (zucchini)
olive oil
salt and pepper

dressing
1 garlic clove, finely chopped
2 tablespoons balsamic vinegar
olive oil

1. Preheat the grill (broiler). Grill (broil) the peppers until their skins begin to blacken. Put them in a bowl and cover. When cool, peel off the skins and deseed. If you are using frozen peppers, simply remove the skin.

2. Using a mandoline, slice the aubergine and courgettes into strips about 1 mm thick. If the aubergine isn't firm enough to slice using a mandoline, use a knife. Drizzle generously with olive oil and season with salt and pepper.

3. Cook the vegetable strips in a single layer in a very hot griddle pan or under the grill. Allow about 2 minutes on each side.

4. Leave the grilled vegetables to cool slightly, then cut the aubergine strips in half lengthways. Cut the peppers into strips.

5. Put all the vegetables in a large bowl, add the garlic and balsamic vinegar and toss to combine. Adjust the seasoning if necessary with a little olive oil, salt and pepper. Serve warm or cold.

waldorf salad

2 chicken breasts, halved horizontally
salt and pepper
6 celery sticks, cut into 5 cm (2 in) lengths
1 small celeriac
1 red apple
2 Little Gem lettuces, leaves separated
1 tablespoon vegetable oil

dressing
60 g (2 oz) natural yoghurt
1 egg yolk
1 tablespoon mustard
juice of ½ lemon
90 ml (3 fl oz) vegetable oil

1. For the dressing, whisk the yoghurt, egg yolk, mustard and lemon juice together. Gradually drizzle in the oil, continuing to whisk as though making mayonnaise. When all the oil has been incorporated, season and set aside.

2. Season the chicken with salt and pepper. Add the remaining tablespoon of oil to a frying pan (skillet) and heat. Add the chicken and sear on both sides. Set aside.

3. Using a mandoline, slice the celery lengthways into ribbons. Place in a bowl of iced water to keep fresh; the ribbons will begin to curl slightly.

4. Peel the celeriac, shred using a julienne peeler and put into a bowl. To keep the pieces as long as possible, turn the peeler around the celeriac as though peeling an apple.

5. Drain the celery ribbons and add to the bowl with the shredded celeriac. Pour over some of the sauce and toss to combine.

6. Thinly slice the chicken. Shred the (unpeeled) apple using a julienne peeler. Divide the lettuce leaves, shredded celeriac and celery, sliced chicken and shredded apple between four plates and serve with the remaining sauce.

coleslaw with maple syrup
and cranberries

¼ white cabbage
¼ red cabbage
200 g (7 oz) carrots
2 spring onions (scallions)
80 g (2½ oz) cranberries

vinaigrette
120 ml (4 fl oz) cider vinegar
90 ml (3½ fl oz) sunflower oil
75 ml (3 fl oz) maple syrup
salt and pepper

1. Using a mandoline, shred the cabbage quarters as finely as possible. Peel the carrots, then shred using a julienne peeler or spiralizer. Finely slice the spring onions and set aside the green parts.

2. Prepare the vinaigrette by mixing together the vinegar, oil and maple syrup. Season with salt and pepper.

3. Put all the vegetables in a large salad bowl, add the cranberries and pour over the vinaigrette. Toss to combine and adjust the seasoning as needed. Scatter with the green parts of the onion.

Chef's tip
Replace the cranberries with raisins if you wish.

chicory and pear with roquefort

2 heads of white chicory
2 heads of red chicory
1 pear
120 g (4 oz) Roquefort

vinaigrette
4 tablespoons walnut oil
3 tablespoons sherry vinegar
salt and pepper

1. For the vinaigrette, mix together the oil and vinegar and season with salt and pepper.

2. Cut each chicory head into quarters lengthways, then slice into long ribbons using a mandoline. Slice the pear into thin strips using a julienne peeler fitted with a wide julienne blade. Crumble the Roquefort into small pieces.

3. Put the chicory ribbons into a bowl, pour over the vinaigrette and add the Roquefort. Toss to combine and divide among four plates. Top each plate with a quarter of the pear strips. Serve immediately.

thai-style papaya and carrot salad

1 small firm papaya
2 large carrots
1 bunch of coriander (cilantro),
leaves picked

dressing
100 g (3½ oz) caster (superfine) sugar
3 tablespoons fish sauce
juice of 2 small lemons
2 garlic cloves, coarsely chopped
1 bird's eye chilli (optional), deseeded
and finely sliced or chopped
salt

1. To make the dressing, dissolve the sugar in the fish sauce and lemon juice. Add the garlic and chilli. Taste and add a little salt if necessary.

2. Peel the papaya and carrots and shred lengthways using a julienne peeler.

3. Dress them with the sauce and serve scattered with a few coriander leaves.

Chef's tips

This salad is great served with prawns (shrimp) or a very thin omelette cut into strips.

For a less sweet sauce, replace half the sugar with agave syrup.

beetroot with fresh goat's cheese
and basil

2 raw red beetroot (beets)
2 raw Chioggia beetroot (beets)
100 g (3½ oz) fresh goat's cheese,
broken into pieces
½ bunch of basil, leaves picked and torn
if large

vinaigrette
4 tablespoons olive oil
4 tablespoons balsamic vinegar
salt and pepper

1. Peel the beetroot and shred using a julienne peeler fitted with a fine julienne blade. Turn the beetroot as you peel them, as though peeling an apple, to get the longest strips possible.

2. Mix together the oil and vinegar and season with salt and pepper.

3. Pour the vinaigrette over the beetroot and toss to combine, then scatter over the goat's cheese and basil.

asparagus tagliatelle
with boiled eggs and parmesan

3 eggs
1 bunch of asparagus
20 g (¾ oz) Parmesan shavings (optional)

vinaigrette
1 small shallot, finely chopped
2 tablespoons white wine vinegar
2 tablespoons olive oil
salt and pepper

1. For the vinaigrette, mix together the shallot, vinegar and oil in a bowl. Season with salt and pepper. Set aside.

2. Plunge the eggs into a pan of boiling water and cook for about 6 minutes. Place the eggs into cold water, then peel them.

3. Wash the asparagus and trim the hard part of the stem. Using a mandoline, slice the asparagus lengthways into strips about 1 mm thick. Blanch in salted boiling water for no more than 1 minute, then drain.

4. Dress the asparagus with the vinaigrette, tossing well to combine. Serve with the boiled eggs and sprinkle with Parmesan shavings if desired.

carrots with orange and spices

4 oranges
1 garlic clove, finely chopped
1 tablespoon honey
1 tablespoon coriander seeds
½ teaspoon allspice (black pepper, nutmeg, clove, cinnamon)
1 bunch of baby carrots
5 tablespoons olive oil
salt
½ bunch of coriander (cilantro), leaves picked

1. Squeeze the oranges and sieve the juice. Pour the juice into a sauté pan, add the garlic, honey, coriander seeds and allspice and heat over a medium heat until reduced by half.

2. Peel the carrots and slice lengthways into strips about 1.5 mm thick using a mandoline.

3. Add the olive oil and carrots to the sauté pan and season with salt.

4. Increase the heat, stir to coat the carrots in the jus and cook until they are tender but still have some bite, about 10 minutes.

5. Serve the carrots hot, at room temperature or cold, sprinkled with coriander leaves.

prawn *bún bò huế*

16 frozen peeled prawns (shrimp)
4 garlic cloves, roughly chopped
salt and pepper
400 g (14 oz) rice vermicelli
2 carrots, peeled
1 small cucumber
200 g (7 oz) beansprouts
1 head of lettuce (e.g. Batavia), leaves roughly chopped
½ bunch of mint, leaves picked
½ bunch of coriander (cilantro), leaves picked
1 tablespoon plain (all-purpose) flour
vegetable oil for frying
50 g (2 oz) peanuts, chopped (optional)

sauce
100 g (3½ oz) caster (superfine) sugar
3 tablespoons fish sauce
juice of 2 lemons
salt
1 bird's eye chilli (optional), deseeded and finely chopped
1 garlic clove, finely chopped

1. Put the prawns in a bowl with the garlic. Season with a little salt and a generous quantity of pepper. Set aside to marinate.

2. Cook the rice vermicelli according to the packet instructions. Drain, rinse under cold water, then drain again.

3. Prepare the sauce. Dissolve the sugar in the fish sauce and lemon juice. Add a little salt if necessary. Add the garlic and chilli and mix well.

4. Shred the carrots and cucumber using a julienne peeler or spiralizer.

5. Divide the beansprouts, vermicelli, cucumber, carrot, lettuce, mint and coriander leaves among four bowls.

6. Preheat a deep-fat fryer to 180°C (350°F). Dry the prawns using kitchen paper, then coat them in the flour, shaking to remove any excess. Sear the prawns in the hot oil for no longer than 1 minute. Drain them on kitchen paper and divide among the bowls.

7. Drizzle over the sauce, sprinkle with the chopped peanuts (if desired) and serve immediately.

Chef's tips

In the traditional recipe, the shells of the prawns are cut but not removed and then coated and seared. This crispy version of *bún bò Huế* uses ready-peeled prawn tails.

If you have any sauce left over, store it in an airtight container in the fridge and serve with carrot salad or spring rolls.

butternut squash tart
with coconut and curry

100 g (3½ oz) butter
6–8 sheets of filo pastry
400 g (14 oz) butternut squash
6 eggs, beaten
20 g (¾ oz) red curry paste
1 × 400 ml (14 fl oz) tin coconut milk
1 teaspoon caster (superfine) sugar
salt

1. Preheat the oven to 180°C (350°F/Gas 4). Melt the butter in the microwave.

2. Using a pastry brush, brush a filo pastry sheet with the melted butter. Use it to line a rectangular mould of about 28 × 20 cm (12 × 8 in). Repeat with the remaining filo sheets, laying them over each other in the mould until you have a solid base with no gaps. Brush a little more melted butter around the edges. Set aside.

3. Peel and deseed the butternut squash then shred the flesh using a julienne peeler fitted with a fine julienne blade. Set aside.

4. Mix the curry paste and coconut milk together, then add the eggs, sugar and a little salt.

5. Lay the butternut spaghetti in the mould then pour over the curry mixture. Put the tin in the oven and leave to cook for about 50 minutes. The tart is cooked when the edges are golden and the egg mixture is set. Turn out onto a wire rack.

vegetable spaghetti nests

2 courgettes (zucchini)
2 carrots, peeled
1 black radish or 1 small daikon, peeled
3 tablespoons vegetable oil
2 garlic cloves, coarsely chopped
2 tablespoons oyster sauce
salt

1. Shred the courgettes, carrots and black radish or daikon using a spiralizer. To keep the pieces as long as possible, turn the vegetables slowly and steadily.

2. Heat the oil in a wok over a high heat. Fry the garlic for a few seconds until golden, then add the shredded vegetables and the oyster sauce. Season lightly with salt and stir gently to avoid breaking up the vegetables. Cooking will be quick: the vegetables should remain al dente.

3. Remove from the heat and form the vegetable spaghetti into small nests by rolling them around a fork. Serve immediately with Thai rice or to accompany fish.

primavera spaghetti

200 g (7 oz) cherry tomatoes
2 garlic cloves, coarsely chopped
salt and pepper
olive oil
300 g (11 oz) asparagus
500 g (1 lb 2 oz) fresh egg spaghetti
150 g (5 oz) fresh shelled (or frozen) peas
grated Parmesan, to serve (optional)

1. Wash and quarter the cherry tomatoes.

2. Put the tomatoes and garlic in a large bowl, season with salt and pepper and drizzle generously with olive oil. Set aside.

3. Trim the hard part of the asparagus stem, then shred the asparagus using a julienne peeler.

4. Cook the spaghetti in salted boiling water according to the packet instructions. Add the peas for the last 5 minutes of the cooking time. When the pasta and peas are al dente, remove the pan from the heat, add the shredded asparagus and stir to combine. Drain immediately.

5. Pour everything over the marinated tomatoes and toss to combine. Adjust the seasoning and finish with a good drizzle of olive oil. Serve with a little grated Parmesan (if desired).

Chef's tip

This dish can also be served cold. Simply rinse the spaghetti in cold water, drain well and tip over the marinated tomatoes.

spiralized cucumber with haddock
and maple syrup vinaigrette

2 cucumbers
300 g (11 oz) smoked haddock, cut into slices
100 g (3½ oz) feta, broken into small pieces
rye bread, to serve (optional)

vinaigrette
1 tablespoon wholegrain mustard
1 tablespoon maple syrup
juice of 1 small lemon
4 tablespoons vegetable oil
a few sprigs of dill, leaves picked and chopped
salt and pepper

1. Make the vinaigrette by mixing together the mustard, maple syrup, lemon juice and oil. Stir in the dill and season to taste.

2. Shred the cucumbers into spaghetti using a spiralizer or julienne peeler. Form the cucumber spaghetti into small nests by rolling around a fork.

3. To serve, lay a few slices of haddock on each plate, top with a cucumber nest, then drizzle over the vinaigrette and scatter over a few pieces of feta. Serve with rye bread.

Chef's tip

The haddock can be substituted with smoked trout or salmon.

julienned vegetables with clams

600 g (1 lb 3 oz) clams
1 courgette (zucchini)
½ onion
2 garlic cloves, coarsely chopped
olive oil
½ teaspoon chilli flakes
salt and pepper
150 ml (5 fl oz) white wine
250 g (9 oz) linguine or spaghetti
1 small tomato, halved, deseeded and diced
a few sprigs of flat-leaf parsley, leaves finely chopped

1. Soak the clams in cold water for 10 minutes, then wash and rinse thoroughly. Discard any open shells.

2. Shred the courgette into long, thin strips using a julienne peeler fitted with a thin julienne blade.

3. Sauté the onion and garlic in a good quantity of olive oil. Add the chilli and season with salt and pepper. Deglaze the pan with the white wine and reduce for 5 minutes.

4. Meanwhile, cook the pasta for 2 minutes less than the time indicated on the packet.

5. Stir the clams and the diced tomato into the sauce. Add the pasta and courgettes, drizzle with olive oil and finish cooking for 2 minutes in the sauce. The pasta should be al dente and the clams open.

6. Serve sprinkled with chopped parsley.

courgette spaghetti
with prawns and garlic

4–5 tablespoons olive oil
3 garlic cloves
zest and juice of ½ lemon
pinch of Espelette pepper
salt
20 peeled raw prawns (shrimp)
5 courgettes (zucchini)
125 g (4½ oz) cherry tomatoes, halved
a few basil leaves

1. Mix together 2 tablespoons of the olive oil, 1 finely chopped garlic clove, the lemon zest, a pinch of Espelette pepper and a pinch of salt. Pour over the prawns and leave to marinate for 10 minutes.

2. Meanwhile, shred the courgettes using a julienne peeler or a spiralizer.

3. Finely chop the remaining garlic cloves. Heat 2 tablespoons of olive oil in a frying pan (skillet). Sauté the courgette spaghetti with the garlic for 2 minutes over a high heat. Season with salt and pepper. Set aside.

4. Sauté the prawns for a few minutes in the same pan. Set aside. Add some more oil to the pan if necessary and stir-fry the cherry tomatoes until golden, then deglaze with the lemon juice and 2 tablespoons of water.

5. Return everything to the pan and reheat quickly. Serve with the basil leaves.

sweet potato tagliatelle
with curry and coconut

2 sweet potatoes
1 x 350 g (12 oz) jar Madras curry sauce
100 ml (3½ fl oz) coconut milk
½ bunch of coriander (cilantro),
leaves picked
juice of ½ lime
chapatis or basmati rice, to serve
(optional)

1. Peel the sweet potatoes, then slice into strips using the tagliatelle blade of a spiralizer. (Alternatively, you could use a julienne peeler, but the tagliatelle will be much shorter.) Set aside.

2. Heat the curry sauce in a pan and add the coconut milk and 200 ml (7 fl oz) water. Add the sweet potato tagliatelle to the sauce and cook over a medium heat for 10–15 minutes. Taste to check that the tagliatelle is done.

3. Just before serving, add the coriander leaves and lime juice. Serve with chapatis or basmati rice.

soba and leek noodles
with salmon

1 leek, two thirds of green leaves removed
1 thumb-sized piece of ginger
dash of vegetable oil
300 g (11 oz) salmon fillet
salt
200 g (7 oz) soba noodles
1 tablespoon toasted sesame seeds
wasabi, to serve

sauce
1 tablespoon demerara sugar
2 tablespoons soy sauce
2 tablespoons sesame oil
juice of ½ lemon

1. Prepare the sauce by mixing together the sugar, soy sauce, sesame oil and lemon juice in a bowl. Set aside.

2. Cut the leek in half horizontally and, holding each half flat, shred using a mandoline into long thin noodles. Finish using a knife if the leek will no longer pass through the mandoline. Set aside.

3. Peel the ginger and shred into thin strips using the mandoline. Cut these ginger strips into juliennes and fry in hot oil. When golden, drain on kitchen paper. Set aside.

4. Season the salmon with salt and stir-fry quickly over a high heat for about 1 minute on each side. The salmon should remain dark pink in the centre. Leave to cool, then cut the fillet into slices 1 cm (½ in) thick.

5. Cook the soba noodles in boiling water according to the packet instructions. Just before the soba noodles are cooked, tip the leek noodles into the pan, then drain. Plunge into cold water to remove the starch then drain again. Pour over the sauce and toss to combine.

6. Divide the soba and leek noodles between two plates and add some slices of salmon next to them. Sprinkle the noodles with the toasted sesame seeds and the salmon with the stir-fried ginger. Serve with a little wasabi.

kohlrabi and turnip spaghetti
with salmon

1 kohlrabi or cabbage
2 swedes
1 shallot, finely chopped
2 tablespoons crème fraîche
2 × 200 g (7 oz) salmon steaks
salt and pepper

1. Preheat the oven to 200°C (400°F/Gas 6). Cut two pieces of baking parchment, each large enough to contain half the ingredients.

2. Peel the kohlrabi or cabbage and swedes, then shred using a julienne peeler fitted with a fine julienne blade. Turn the blade around the vegetable, as though peeling an apple, to keep the pieces as long as possible.

3. Place half the chopped shallot in the centre of one of the squares of parchment. Add a tablespoon of crème fraîche, then top with a salmon steak. Season with salt and pepper. Cover with half the vegetable spaghetti and season again.

4. Close the parcel by bringing the edges of the paper together, folding them tightly to seal and upwards to ensure there are no leakages. Repeat to make the second parcel. Cook in the oven for 10–15 minutes. Serve hot.

aubergine and tagliatelle
with tomato sauce

1 large firm aubergine (eggplant)
100 ml (3½ fl oz) olive oil
salt and pepper
500 g (1 lb 2 oz) fresh tagliatelle
1 bunch of basil, leaves picked and torn
if large

tomato sauce
5 tablespoons olive oil
1 onion, finely chopped
2 garlic cloves, coarsely chopped
2 sprigs of thyme
1½ × 400 g (14 oz) tins chopped tomatoes
pinch of caster (superfine) sugar
salt and pepper

1. Prepare the tomato sauce. Heat the oil in a pan, add the onion and sauté over a low heat. Add the garlic and thyme, then the tomatoes and sugar. Season with salt and pepper. Leave to stew over a low heat for about 20 minutes. Set aside.

2. Meanwhile, slice the aubergine into strips using a julienne peeler fitted with a wide julienne blade.

3. Heat the oil in a large frying pan (skillet) and lay the aubergine strips flat into the pan. Season with salt and pepper. Cook for 5 minutes on each side until golden. Drain on kitchen paper and set aside.

4. Cook the tagliatelle in a pan of salted boiling water according to the packet instructions. Drain and mix with the hot tomato sauce (reheat the sauce first if necessary). Add the aubergine and mix together. Scatter the basil leaves over the top to serve.

shredded runner beans
with tomato sauce

400 g (14 oz) runner beans (green beans)
2 tablespoons olive oil
a few flat-leaf parsley leaves, chopped

tomato sauce
5 tablespoons olive oil
½ onion
1 garlic clove, finely chopped
1 sprig of thyme
1 × 400 g (14 oz) tin chopped tomatoes
pinch of caster (superfine) sugar
salt and pepper

1. Prepare the tomato sauce. Heat the oil in a pan, add the onion and sauté over a low heat. Add the garlic and thyme, then the tomatoes and sugar. Season with salt and pepper. Leave to stew over a low heat for about 15 minutes. Set aside.

2. Wash the beans. Shred them by slicing them lengthways using a mandoline. Set aside.

3. Bring a pan of water to the boil and cook the runner beans for 5 minutes. Drain and set aside.

4. Reheat the tomato sauce and add the beans and olive oil. Stir and cook together for a few minutes. The beans can be slightly crunchy or well-cooked, depending on your preference. If you prefer the latter, leave them to cook for a little longer.

5. Serve hot, warm or cold, sprinkled with chopped parsley.

potato carbonara

3 large potatoes, peeled
8 rashers of streaky bacon
500 ml (16 fl oz) crème fraîche
20 g (¾ oz) Parmesan, grated (optional)
1 small garlic clove, finely chopped
salt and pepper
2 egg yolks, lightly beaten

1. Cut the potatoes into long strips using a spiralizer.

2. Bring a large pan of salted water to the boil. Add the potato spaghetti and cook for about 10 minutes. Taste to check that they are done.

3. Meanwhile, fry the bacon in a non-stick frying pan (skillet) until beginning to crisp. Set aside.

4. Heat the crème fraîche in the same pan, then add the Parmesan (if desired) and garlic. Season with salt and pepper. Reduce for a few minutes, then add the egg yolks. Stir and leave to thicken over a low heat.

5. Once cooked, carefully drain the potato spaghetti. The strands break easily so handle with care.

6. Arrange the potato spaghetti on the plates. Pour over the sauce and top each plate with two rashers of crispy bacon.

steak and chips with a twist

3 large, long potatoes
1 tablespoon sunflower oil
1 thick sirloin steak (450 g/1 lb)
salt
vegetable oil, for frying

béarnaise sauce
1 shallot, finely chopped
2 tablespoons white wine
2 tablespoons vinegar
2 sprigs of tarragon, leaves picked and
snipped
1 egg yolk
60 g (2 oz) cold butter, diced
salt and pepper

1. Prepare the béarnaise sauce. Put the shallot in a pan with the white wine, vinegar and tarragon and reduce until almost all the liquid has evaporated, then turn the heat down to its lowest setting. Add the egg yolk and 1 tablespoon of water and season with salt and pepper. Whisk, scraping down the edges of the pan. As soon as the mixture has thickened, add the butter in three stages, continuing to whisk. Set aside.

2. Shred the potatoes spaghetti-thin using a spiralizer. (You may need to trim the potato first if its diameter exceeds that of the spiralizer.) Set aside.

3. Heat the sunflower oil in a frying pan (skillet). Sprinkle the steak with salt, then sear it in the oil over a high heat. For a rare steak, allow about 2 minutes on each side. Transfer to a grill rack to rest.

4. Meanwhile, cook the spiralized potato in a deep-fat fryer at 180°C (350°F). When it is golden, drain, then sprinkle with salt.

5. Serve the spiralized potato immediately with the steak and béarnaise sauce.

Super Spiralized by Orathay Souksisavanh & Vania Nikolcic

First published in 2010 by Hachette Books (Marabout)
This English hardback edition published in 2017 by Hardie Grant Books

Hardie Grant Books (UK)
52-54 Southwark Street
London SE1 1UN
hardiegrant.co.uk

Hardie Grant Books (Australia)
Ground Floor, Building 1
658 Church Street
Melbourne, VIC 3121
hardiegrant.com.au

British Library Cataloguing-in-Publication Data. A catalogue
record for this book is available from the British Library.

ISBN: 978-1-78488-102-3

For the English hardback edition:
Publisher: Kate Pollard
Senior Editor: Kajal Mistry
Editorial Assistant: Hannah Roberts
Translator and Copy Editor: Anne McDowell
Colour Reproduction by p2d

Printed and bound in China by 1010

10 9 8 7 6 5 4 3 2 1